Deciding to Love

Turn Your Argumentative, Frustrating, Painful Relationship into An Understanding, Healthy, Happy, Loving Relationship

PATRICK AND RAINIE HOWARD

Also by Rainie Howard:

ADDICTED TO PAIN

YOU ARE ENOUGH

WHEN GOD SENT MY HUSBAND

UNDENIABLE BREAKTHROUGH

MIRACLES IN YOUR MOUTH

Howard Global Enterprises Publishing Agency

For information about special discounts for bulk purchases or bringing the author to your live event, please contact Rainie Howard Enterprises Sales
at 314-827-5216 or Contact@RainieHoward.com
Manufactured in the United State of America

ISBN: 978-1-7340155-8-4

DEDICATION

———— ❧❦❧ ————

This book is dedicated to everyone seeking a healthy, happy loving relationship.

TABLE OF CONTENTS

—————— ❦❧ ——————

INTRODUCTION

It felt like a fairytale, after dreaming of finding love, hoping to one day be in love and visualizing experiencing love; I finally owned love. That love was my living reality. It wasn't just any kind of love but a deep love coexisting with a friendship of devotion. The love was so deep that it increased my fears. My fear of losing what I finally had and always desired became overwhelming. The spine-chilling thoughts of another woman's seduction and wittiness alluring my man was haunting my mind. The fear of him falling into her temptation, the fear of the pain it may bring, and the fear of losing all the love I desperately lacked for so many years was profoundly engrossing me. I yearned for that love from my deepest inner being, I thirst for it, I craved it and desired it deeply. Oh, I was seething with vindictiveness. That fear of a love lost was creating a savage, ruthless, outrageous woman who would do anything to prevent losing that love. It implicated I needed to control as much as I could. I would use manipulation, threats and pity. I would demand, "show me you love me." I would create scenarios in my mind, "if you ever cheated on me, I'll leave you." We would argue and go back and forth about things that never happened. Fear was the author and finisher of our altercations. I believed by threatening him that I would leave would enforce enough fear that he would barricade his mind from ever thinking about another woman. I wanted to control his mind from ever considering it. And here I was; miserable and vulnerable again.

All those years growing up in a home without my father and leading to my desperation for male attention, love and affection left me miserable. Although finally having my amazing and God-sent loving husband I found myself trapped in misery again. I felt lonely, lost and unwanted again. The once strong passion, desire and determination to make him mine, transformed into a new strong passionate fear and determination to prevent me from losing him. I didn't realize it until years later. But my reckless ways of clinging onto him was subconsciously pushing him further and further away. It seems insane to think that I was pushing the love I so much desired away.

The fear of growing apart was so deeply instilled in my mind that I insistently tried to make sure we agreed on deep conversations that were important to me. When we disagreed it often led to another big blow up altercation. Instead of me focusing on self-care and personal growth, my fears and insecurities steered me to a dark place of emptiness and for years I lost myself in the position and role as his wife.

There were seasons when I became passionate about other things like business goals, and mission projects; but most of the time my business engagement was the result of the realization that I couldn't control him. I couldn't force him to focus on me every day and all day, and out of spite and resentment I became busy. I decided to no longer nag, beg and cry about him not spending enough time with me and to no longer expect his pity when convincing him that my love language was quality time. The threats would bounce back as a form of manipulation, "I don't feel loved because my love language is quality time and that is not what I'm getting from you."

As these feeble arguments bore no fruit, I made up my mind to become too busy for him to cope with it. And hopefully, and maybe he would notice and come begging for my attention and love. It was intentional. I told myself, "don't be needy, be busy." It worked for a while until I became overwhelmingly stressed and burned out due to an overload of work. I was trying to prove a point but after months going by and with my desperate heart that couldn't take it anymore another blow up argument would unleash. And here we were back again yelling at each other, mad and frustrated, both realizing that this is the same argument we've been having for years. We thought that argument was buried, gone and dead but it struck back with a vengeance.

I didn't know or understand at the time that I was being manipulative, controlling and that I needed to change. I was in a very low point of my life and I thought he was largely to be blamed for my unhappiness. He hadn't planned any dates, romantic get-a-ways or initiated sex in a while. I was the one planning dates, planning get-a-way trips and we had sex only when I initiated it. I told him something needed to change, or our marriage would suffer the devastation of a separation. Yes separation, that's the word I felt comfortable using after experiencing a big tantrum enraged outburst from him when using the word 'divorce' during an argument when we were a newlywed couple. I wanted to threaten him without triggering an overwhelming rage and anger in him. I knew from experience what his weakness was. He didn't want to lose me either, but he did not seem to understand why I was so unhappy.

The mutual misunderstanding frustrated us both. We both wanted answers but the more we talked about it the lousier it made us both feel. So, most of the time we decided to ignore it. We simply kept on tricking ourselves into believing things would somehow get better because we had love.

Love Misunderstood

For the longest time I've known, I've never wanted to be that old man still chasing after women in search of a relationship. I refused to be that old guy offering to pay woman's utility bills, reeking in the cologne of my younger years. I wanted a long term, stable and loving relationship while I was young. The type of relationship I desired was unlike any I had seen. I was used to seeing toxic, unhealthy and dysfunctional relationships. Dysfunction was so common it seemed normal. Nevertheless, I was determined not to allow myself to fall prey to the same strongholds that plagued so many relationships around me. As my own defense mechanism to avoid the shortcomings in the dysfunctional relationships I was accustomed to, I developed a simple strategy as to how I would excel in a relationship. My simple strategy was aimed at all behavior I saw that brought about shame and negative results; I would just set my mind on doing the opposite. For example, some men were serious alcoholics, so I would make a deliberate decision to never touch alcohol. Some men were verbally abusive to their wives and girlfriends whenever they got angry, so I would intentionally not to be verbally abusive to my spouse or girlfriend if in a rage of anger. And some men were just not present at all, leaving mothers to fulfill the role of both father and mother for their children. Therefore, I would make a decision from my heart to always be there for my family regardless of any conflicts.

Adopting this kind of strategy seemed like the best way to address conflict, but I would soon find out it was indeed a shortsighted one. My main assumption was as long as I wasn't like "them" I was better. I believed this would help me lead a better life and have the long and stable loving relationship I truly desired. I convinced myself that by fully implementing this strategy, there was nothing left for me to work on and that I had everything figured out. All I needed now was the relationship to provide it. Yet, I was so wrong.

The truth was I had instead become very prideful and overly competitive with an ambitious goal of surviving dysfunction without actually knowing how to address conflicts. I didn't really know how to respond when I got angry and I didn't know the true meaning of being present for my family. I simply knew what I did NOT want my relationship to look like. At the same time, I subconsciously lowered my expectations for the elements required to lead a lifelong loving relationship. The fact that these questions remained unanswered, resulted in recurring conflicts throughout my relationship and I was forced to face them whether I deemed it necessary or not.

At this point, God has led me to find the love of my life. My crown, my wife, my virtuous woman. This woman had been overlooked by men who hesitated to commit to her because they were intimidated by her strength and determination. Not me. I have never been intimated by a beautiful and strong woman. I saw her strength and her commitment to her goals in life and it reminded me a bit of myself. She's beautiful, knows what she wants out of life and is dedicated to her ambition to bring about the desires of her heart. This to me was very sexy. Her being a strong-willed woman excited me and I knew I was what she needed. In fact, I thought in line with the strategy I've perfected, I considered it a blessing bestowed on her to be with me.

In my mind, I was everything she would want in a man as I knew exactly what I would be to her. I would be the best provider, friend and husband she could ever imagine having. Filled with the pride of knowing I had everything needed to make a relationship work, I did not doubt the potential of this relationship for one minute. And I was confident I would gift her with lasting happiness. I however would soon learn to effectively manage the seasons of change that come in a marriage; one cannot come from a place of pride to share and show love. The foundation and starting point should be love.

So here I am; convinced I am mentally prepared to enjoy the best relationship, overly busy navigating my career while trying to make sure I was present and available. And here is where I end up; receiving harsh criticism for not showing love, being disconnected and not being present. Not to mention I didn't take criticism very well. And because I never effectively learned how to resolve conflicts, I put in every effort to avoid them. This would quieten me down during the start of confronting conversations, in an attempt to seem agreeable, until my lack of communication and resentment combined with feeling unappreciated caused my emotions to boil over into a rage filled outburst. My goal had always been to control my anger but the more criticism I received the angrier I got. Did my pride turn me into a cold-hearted beast, or was my wife merely trying to control me? I wasn't sure but the thought of ending up in a dysfunctional and bad relationship haunted my mind. I wanted to avoid it as much as I could, that plague was burdensome. For the sake of my pride and an outward act of humility, I would reluctantly take heed to the criticism whether I deemed it warranted or not and tried to take actions to resolve the conflict. I had become a bit of a fixer, with the heavy weight of our relationship on my shoulders. Though I was not solely responsible for this burden, I was determined not to be the cause of the relationship falling apart due to a lack of presence on my part. Nevertheless, I was confident that my presence alone should count as a major act of love, considering we both grew up in single parent homes. My sheer presence combined with all else I've already done should exceed the poor performance of the father figures who should have been present in our own lives.

Overtime, the unaddressed built up feelings of being unappreciated along with resentment combined with the pressures of life caused me to feel burnt out. I no longer wanted to play the guessing game. I had to face the truth and the truth was I didn't know what to do. For so long, I had focused on how things looked instead of evaluating how things truly were. I became withdrawn from the intimacy required in a loving relationship. I needed to take a serious inward look and address why I experienced so much resentment. Now was the time to develop the proper strategies and figure out how to operate from a place of love and not pride, for me to be a more complete and happy man.

The truth was, the philosophy I focused on implementing towards my success, was based on my fear not to be like the failed relationships and flawed people I had seen. This was a misinterpreted view of what it looked like to love. Ultimately, I was using pride to mask my fear of failure and the fear of becoming like the men I had seen while growing up. Consequently, my pride and fear of failure caused me to take criticism far too personally. I had given the power of being responsible for my own happiness away. I furthermore took the notion of a happy wife and happy life literally to the point where I felt responsible for my wife's happiness. Now knowing that I cannot control the happiness of others, I needed to learn to love freely and unconditionally without fear of failure masked in pride and performance. Love covers a multitude of shortcomings, including our own. We must love ourselves enough to freely be who God created us to be and allow others to do the same. When you love life and appreciate every moment God has given you, you are able to acknowledge that the place God brought you from was necessary to develop the strength you need for today. We are not called to carry the burden where we come from, but we are to acknowledge the blessings that come from overcoming its vices unashamed.

What is supposed to be love in those rare moments actually feels more like pain. You're supposed to be happy and, on the outside, everything looks good, but the truth is deep down inside you are wondering if it will last.

What do you do when the love fades, when the commitment wavers and when you're not sure if you will stay in a relationship? How do you endure the challenges of the heart and the feelings of frustration that makes you want to quit? How do you get through the hurtful emotions, the resentment and the fears that hold you hostage? How do you stop replaying the disappointing past that seems to define your present moment?

But yes, you do really love him. It's just chaotic at times. Most days things are calm and smooth. But then comes the stormy times when the wrong button is pushed and the atmosphere changes, to such an extent that you don't recognize him anymore. He becomes a stranger to you. You don't recognize yourself anymore, you're shaken up and fearful. You're confused and uncertain of what's next. You don't know why things blow up so badly and the rage, pain and anger get out of control. Where does it come from? Where has it been hiding all the time and when will it make a comeback? Will the next time be worse?

CHAPTER 1

⁓⁓⁓⁓⁓

TRAUMATIC EMOTIONS OF REJECTION

It's the bickering, criticism and frustrating disagreements that gets to you. Why can't he understand, why are we always upset with each other? Most of the time we would ignore our frustrations, put on a happy face and distract ourselves, and stay involved with the issues of life. On the outside we looked like a happy fun couple but on the inside the misunderstanding and resentment was pushing us away from each other. At times I questioned myself, "When will we have the next blow up argument?" Things seemed to go well for a while but something petty would happen and we would be at it again. Yelling, crying, arguing and raging. All this caused me to feel desperate, lost and alone. Yes, feeling alone while being married. Feeling alone while being in a long-term committed relationship with years and years of history, memories and experience. Why feel lonely when you are with the love of your life? Why feel lonely when marriage was supposed to cure loneness? Shouldn't I feel fulfilled, whole and complete? I should be happy, right? Well I wasn't happy at all. Here I was with the first man who had ever patiently waited for me. For years he dated me, and we built a strong relationship through the development of friendship and loyalty. I had never experienced that kind of commitment and love in all my life, yet I couldn't understand how a small petty argument (over him being too busy to take me out on dates) can turn into so much pain and resentment. It resulted in me questioning whether or not our marriage would last.

I didn't realize that all of the trauma from my past (including rejection, abandonment and heartbreak) were the biggest threat against my marriage. I wasn't aware that the pain of my past had impacted how I viewed my husband. At that time of my life, I couldn't fathom how to appreciate my husband for the amazing man he is. I could only see his flaws and weaknesses. No one is perfect and if you are mentally programed to find the wrong things in someone, you will surely find them and even more. Every great and amazing person do have flaws and weaknesses and my mind would always be looking for the wrong. I had this distorted belief that when things were going well, something bad was bound to happen. I would often think, "It's too good to be true." That belief pattern made me miserable and paranoid, waiting for the next bad thing to happen even when things were going well.

I now understand when a person has dealt with trauma in their life, biological and chemical changes occur in the brain. These changes can literally shift your life, health, and reality as you know it, by means of the post-traumatic brain.

I realized that my past trauma was one of the main reasons my mind was so focused on everything my husband wasn't doing right. Those past traumas were blocking me from receiving and enjoying my blessings. The truth is, even if you are surrounded by all the love, joy, health and peace you could ever desire but you are filled with hurt, pain and resentment, your life experience will feel void of all the present blessings in your life. Trauma does not go away just because your traumatic experience is now over. Trauma often leaves a "blueprint" on your mind and that blueprint acts as a guide that impacts your experiences.

I remember one evening after my husband and I had a big argument with lots of yelling, anger and emotional turmoil, I noticed that I started experiencing similar feelings to what I felt as a little girl crying and scared after listening to my parents argue and fight. I physically started shacking in fear. The fear of reliving that pain flooded my emotions and I began questioning if my marriage would survive. In that very moment I felt like I was having an anxiety attack. My past painful emotions were evading my present reality. In that moment I stopped observing my husband as the problem. I realized my unresolved feelings and traumatic emotions had a lot to do with my internalized fears. And it dawned on me that I was in desperate need of healing.

In the beginning of my healing process, I learned two profound lessons.

1) I must take full ownership of my emotions and no longer blame my husband for my feelings.
2) I am no longer to take his actions personally.

When my husband would do something that offended me or say something that would hurt my feelings, I would no longer take it personally. I made the decision not to internalize it. I would tell myself, what he did or said has nothing to do with my value as a human. I would not internalize the offense and I would no longer allow the feelings of rejection and disappointment to consume me. I learned to understand that his decisions had nothing to do with my value or self-worth. If I felt myself getting emotional and taking things personally, I would remind myself that my emotions were my responsibility and I could not expect him to be the healer of my emotions. Healing my emotions were my responsibility alone. I stopped feeling like a victim. I stopped playing the blame game and I started taking full ownership of my healing process. This empowered me to gain strength and take my life back. I would no longer cry uncontrollably or feel sorry for myself. I began to discover how strong I have always been, although not acknowledging it until I embarked on the journey of my healing process.

No matter what situation you are dealing with right now it has no power except for the meaning you attach to it. If you observe your situation as big and unbearable, that's exactly what it's bound to become in your life.

A woman was dealing with infidelity in her marriage. It left her angered and depressed. She thought that the infidelity happened because she wasn't pretty enough and because of her weight gain. She blamed herself and kept herself in captivity through her biased personal interpretation of that situation. The infidelity in reality had nothing to do with her but was a personal issue her spouse needed to change in himself.

Be careful not to attach the wrong meaning to the wrong situation. We often label things, give them meaning and then blame others for the outcome of our feelings. We must understand that we have the power and strength to overcome every negative emotion by giving it to God in prayer and letting go of blaming others. We often give people, places and things too much power over our lives.

It's not what people say or do to you that makes you feel disrespected or unloved. It's how you interpret what they said or did that made you feel the way you feel.

When someone says something to you in a negative way, you can either believe they are disrespecting you or you can believe it's not about you, but they are having a bad day and they are feeling unloved. We all know the saying "Hurt people, Hurt people." If they're being hurtful towards you the real meaning is that they are the ones who are hurting. Most people in pain are struggling with an illusion of loss. This is absolutely no excuse to justify and accept bad toxic behavior from people. This is only to help you avoid internalizing toxic behavior as a meaning of your self-worth.

I encourage you to elevate yourself to a higher level of meaning. As you evolve in your level of thinking you can mature to an understanding that you lack nothing. There is no real loss. Everything transforms to a higher level; nothing is a loss.

"Let perseverance finish its work so that you may be mature and complete, not lacking anything." –James 1:4

We must evolve to a higher level of understanding that our worth has nothing to do with the circumstances that happen in life. Being single doesn't mean you're lacking anything. Single means whole. We all came into this world single. Being in a challenging marriage doesn't mean you're lacking love. Being in a toxic relationship doesn't mean you are worthless. How can you lack love when you came from love? God is love and nothing can ever separate you from the love of God. Love dwells inside of you.

Stop allowing your current situation to define you. Raise up into your truth and take ownership of the infinite power of God that dwells within you. You are valuable beyond measure.

When you create an illusion of loss it causes feelings and

emotions of pain. Some people experience different situations considered by others as a major loss like a divorce, the death of a loved one, and the loss of a physical limb. Yet they choose to live a life of joy and peace. Some may wonder, how can they not be living in pain? It's because they decided to elevate to a higher level of meaning and not to allow that situation become their identity.

Don't allow the painful emotions of rejection and abandonment to become your identity. Ask yourself what is the story you've been telling yourself? Is it a story of your past where you were the victim? Do you see yourself as sensitive, weak or broken? Or do you see yourself as the bad guy who doesn't deserve anything good?

The Outcry for Help

Understand that when it comes to communication every response is either a loving response or an outcry for help. Let's think about this. Think about the last disagreement with a loved one; the times when their response was harsh or hostile. If you stopped and really listened with understanding, you could hear the outcry for help. Sometimes that cry is, "I fear losing you, or I'm struggling to trust your love for me, or I feel alone and misunderstood."

You being aware of their outcry for help doesn't justify bad behavior or set you up for a fight. It only reinforces your maturity not to take what they said personally. Stop allowing their words and actions to control you and instead understand it's really not about you.

Your understanding will help you gain control of your emotions, lower your tone of voice and relax your facial expressions, which both play a major role in the value of your communication.

Some people decide not to be understanding and instead become resentful and confrontational. Others avoid talking and silently hold on to their bitter and angry thoughts. In addition to being understanding, it's also important to communicate in a loving and calm way. Never avoid talking and communicating. Make an intentional decision to have the conversation in a tranquil tone, while stopping to listen with the goal to better understand what is being relayed. It's always best to communicate the love and appreciation you have for that individual so that they understand where your heart is. Make a point of repeating what they've said, as proof that you were listening attentively and are trying your best to understand and reconcile the relationship.

It's also important not to judge them or try to change them. Focus on understanding them, being loving and considerate. This requires a humble and willing spirit. You must be willing to let go of pride and resentment. Ask yourself, what's more important? You being right or being in love?

Unfortunately, there are people who are willing to divorce and destroy their relationship just for the sake of being right. Being right and holding on to their pride is more important than being in love and holding on to their relationship.

You must be willing to swallow your pride and do what's best to protect the peace and love in your relationship.

JOURNAL

How does the trauma from your past (including rejection, abandonment and heartbreak) impact your relationship?

_____

_____

_____

_____

_____

We often tell ourselves a story why we do what we do and often blame life circumstances as the reason for our disappointment and failure. What is the story you've been telling yourself?

_____

_____

_____

_____

_____

Do you see yourself as sensitive, weak or broken? Or do you see yourself as the bad guy who doesn't deserve anything good?

_____

_____

_____

_____

_____

What's more important? To be right or to be in love?

_____

_____

_____

_____

_____

"No matter what situation you are dealing with right now it has no power but the meaning you give it."

CHAPTER 2

—————— ✍❧✍❧ ——————

LEARNING THE LESSON

When people do you wrong and repetitiously mistreat you, instead of taking revenge and becoming angry make the decision to learn a lesson from your experience. There is always a lesson for you to learn. If you are willing to pay close attention, you will be able to find a lesson and that lesson will always serve you. When avoiding learning the lessons in life, you remain in the pain and often attract accelerated pain. Never resist knowing the truth, even if the truth may hurt. The truth will guide you to making wise decisions. Resistance will keep you stuck in pain. Learn the lesson by surrendering to what is. Face the fact head on; you are actually stronger than you think. If you keep avoiding the truth and neglecting to learn the lesson, life will keep putting you through the same test with tougher and more painful results until you finally get it.

There are things in life you will desire but if you miss learning the lessons in your life you will not be ready for what you truly desire. The gifts you receive in life are equivalent to the person you become. Enjoying a healthy and happy relationship requires you to become a healthy and happy person. How can you expect to experience an amazing fulfilling relationship while you're lonely and miserable? Do you think someone is going to come along and heal you from the inside out and transform your life in a relationship? No, it will not happen. Your healing is your own responsibility. God has given you all the power and authority to apply His wisdom to heal yourself.

Jessica always felt an emptiness in her life. She yearned for love and affection from men and men desired her. They loved her beauty, style and the shape of her body. She was alluring. She knew how to easily gain the attention of a man. She would mesmerize him with her flirtatious conversation. Her friends often called her a hopeless romantic because she maintained a new relationship for a brief period. Her love affairs would start very fast and passionate but would often end very fast and cold-hearted.

Jessica would get bored after a while and the relationships would end soon after, accept for her relationship with Frank. Frank was a multi-millionaire who lived in Miami Florida and Jessica lived in Houston Texas. They started dating after meeting at a business convention. There was something different about Frank. Jessica saw something in him that she had never seen in any other relationship. She saw power. Frank walked like power, talked like power, and looked like power. He was a businessman and he was one of the top industry leaders.

Jessica saw a future with Frank. She envisioned their life together living in his mansion, enjoying the lavish life and holding the position as his wife.

Frank would fly Jessica into town, wine and dine her and then treated her to a romantic evening at a five-star luxury hotel. He would tell her how beautiful she looked and how much he loved her. She took it all in, she became so attached to Frank that she couldn't go a moment without thinking about him. She had never felt this way about any man she'd ever dated. Jessica was attached.

She no longer enjoyed her life in Houston as the owner of her boutique. She told her friends she would give it all up and move to Miami to be with Frank. She told Frank she was ready to take their relationship to the next level and move in with him. Frank told Jessica he had something important to share with her. Jessica's heart began to beat faster. Here they were in their favorite restaurant in such a beautiful ambiance finishing a delicious candlelight dinner. Could he be preparing to propose to her? Could he possibly invite her to come and live in his mansion? Frank broke the news. "Jessica, I love you with all my heart and I want to spend the rest of my life with you. I see us traveling the world together, having children and creating a legacy of love. You are the only woman I want in my life, but I have something very important to tell you. I'm at the end of a very rocky and dark relationship and my ex girlfriend is currently living in my house."

In one moment, the tears of joy filling Jessica's eyes quickly turned into tears of pain. Jessica froze, she couldn't move. She didn't know what to say, all she could do is cry. Her heart was broken. Frank put his arm around her and said, "Baby, I love you. Soon all of this will be over, and she will be out of my house. I just wanted to be honest with you because I'm ready for us to move to the next level of our love relationship. But I need to know that you are committed and prepared to get through this with me."

Jessica sadly nodded her head and passively said, "Yes, I'm willing to get through this with you. It had been seven months since Jessica and Frank were dating and she had never seen his house. She thought Frank lived alone and they spent most of their time together in hotels because the location was closer to his companies. She was shocked to find out another woman was living with her man.

Instead of being upset with Frank for keeping that from her for so long she was upset with herself for crying and being so emotional. "I'm sorry Frank, I love and support you. I'm here for you. I don't know why I'm so emotional." She quickly wiped her eyes and put on a smile. It was a fake smile. All she could think of was, "I've got to be here for him, support him, love him and sacrifice whatever is necessary to be with my man."

Jessica didn't realize it was not love that kept her committed to a toxic relationship, but largely attachment. She was attached. In her mind she was nothing without Frank. She thought she needed him more than anything. He was a big part of how she valued her self-worth.

Attachment is not love; it is nothing else than fear. You were created as a unique whole individual. There is nothing incomplete about you. You are whole and you lack nothing. You have all that you need. Your value is within you. Some marriages are only surviving because of attachment.

Neither person feels that they have a life outside of the relationship and both have become clingy and needy. An attachment relationship can be very unhealthy.

The big issue is the mistake people make looking for self-worth in all the wrong places. Your real love is within. The more you look inside, the more you'll discover God, the Holy Spirit and your inner self. It's in the inner places of your soul and spirit where you discover love in abundance. Once you connect with this kind of love you will find true fulfillment and wholeness. That love will also lead to a deeper and more fulfilled love in your relationship.

Much more is required

As I drove into work listening to a motivational video, the words I heard hit me much harder than usual. Spoken by Bishop T.D. Jakes, "it is possible for life to lead you faster than your mind is prepared to handle. God can move you into a place where positionally you are in a place of leadership but mentally and emotionally you have no grip on what life has handed you. And if you don't know what you have, you don't know how to take care of it."

I listened to this message almost 3 days every week during my morning drive into work. But something was different. It wasn't the words that were spoken that had changed but it was the place I found myself in mentally that caused me to see the same thing differently. In the past, I listened to this statement and thought about my kids and the season of life they were in. But this time I saw myself.

Thinking about this chronicle made me reflect on my relationship and the life I desired and was praying for all along. I desired a relationship that would last a lifetime, a relationship as an example and inspiration to others of how a loving relationship should be. In my moments of desire, I did not realize I was also asking for all of the challenges that comes with such a relationship. And it reminded me of the scripture verse in Luke 12, which states, "to whom much is given, much more is required of him."

The key words that grabbed me were the words 'much more'. I had been operating from the viewpoint that I could do much less and still fulfill my role as a good husband, as I knew better than the men who have lived out their failures before me. My father, uncles and step dad were toxic and they were never present and available for their families. I was nothing like them and therefore I felt my wife had it good with me.

As a matter of fact, considering the sufferings many women had endured by the hands of men, I believed that less conflict meant more value for a woman who desired a peaceful home. Contradictory, and with full understanding of the scripture, the passage is warning us of the fate of two people. Firstly, the fate of the person who understands they have the knowledge and talent to do well. Yet instead of preparing for the challenges ahead and following through with what they know to be right, they do nothing. Secondly, the fate of the person that does not have the knowledge and understanding how they truly ought to be and from that place of ignorance makes the same mistakes. The first person with a better knowledge increases his/her expectations and when the performance does not match the performer, a heightened level of disappointment and consequence manifests. The second person still experiences a level of disappointment and consequences, but knowing that they lack the knowledge and competencies to perform at a certain level, the consequences are not so fierce.

It was clear to me that it was an unrealistic expectation to reach a certain level in my relationship and life without putting in the necessary work and energy to get there. There is no such thing as a guaranteed position of leadership or success in life. It is not the years of service in a particular role that represents how well you are prepared to overcome the conflicts of one level, but it is the commitment, discipline and consistency of overcoming issues that denotes a person's preparedness for the next level of life's challenges.

This is the reason why individuals both married and single, at times, face the same challenges year after year. Issues occur repetitively because the lesson required to effectively address and overcome these challenges has not been learned. Even more so, people don't know who they are and how to be the best person God created them to be. It requires of you becoming your best self despite the examples you've grown up with. My eyes are now opened. I no longer look at others to determine what my success should look like. I now look internally to see how I need to position myself and be prepared for the greatness I desire in my life. At this point, it no longer made sense to hold on to excuses of already being good enough in who I am and what I do. The focus was now on working on things to help me become the person I desired to be. And it all started with me confronting myself and not others.

JOURNAL
———————— ✥❧◈❧ ————————

Have you ever felt lonely while being in a relationship? What do you believe caused the deep feelings of loneliness?

_____

_____

_____

_____

_____

Do you ever blame your partner for your unhappiness? If so, how can you begin to take ownership of your happiness?

_____

_____

_____

_____

_____

"The gifts in life that you receive are equivalent to the person you become. Enjoying a healthy and happy relationship requires you to become a healthy happy person."

CHAPTER 3

———— ❦❦ ————

THE VICTIM AND THE SAVIOR

It's very common for people with a victim mindset to attract people with the savior mentality. The victim is on a constant journey looking for a savior and the savior has a mission to rescue and take responsibility for saving the victim. The victim holds others responsible for his/her personal value and boundaries. The savior takes responsibility for others' values and boundaries while neglecting his/her own personal values and boundaries. Both the victim and the savior have lost their perception of self-validation. One is seeking others to validate himself/herself and the other is seeking to validate others. When it comes to developing healthy relationships, it's very important to know your worth and set boundaries. Knowing your worth has more to do with knowing, accepting and loving yourself and it has absolutely nothing to do with being in a relationship.

The systems and programming of this world teaches you to find your value in people, places and things. The problem with this is when your value and self-worth come from people, places, and things you lose your value when people leave, places fail, and things are taken away.

The victim believes he/she has no control over life and feels helpless. They are programmed to believe that everything wrong in life is someone else's fault. Victims are complainers and blamers. The savior find value in fixing things and rescuing others. They thrive on it if people rely on them. They take responsibility for the behavior of those close to them. They will drop everything in their life just to be there for others. This is very unhealthy.

Can you relate to the victim and savior relationship?

Charles was extremely distressed with his life. He had a low self-esteem and a very hard time keeping a job. He blamed his parents being the reason for him struggling in life. He often alleged his Dad didn't spend enough time with him as a kid and his mom never accepted the women he dated. Charles would get angry about his life and threw big tantrums blaming anyone and everyone for his emotional flare-ups. When Charles met Brittany, things got very serious really fast. Brittany had a savior personality (some may even call her a people pleaser or approval seeker). The savior's personality is never happy when the victim is unhappy. Whenever Charles was upset, and moody Brittany would get depressed. She would do everything in her power to make him happy. She would spend hours trying to cheer him up. She would give him money and take on his responsibilities by paying his bills and calling his job when he wasn't going to show up for work. She gave her all in the relationship while he gave nothing except more complaining and even more blaming. It seemed the more Brittany did for him the more he disrespected her. He cheated on her several times. He even became verbally abusive towards her. Charles had a toxic mentality and was always abusive towards people who loved and cared for him.

Brittany felt stuck. She didn't know what to do. Although she really loved Charles and wanted him to be happy, she felt drained and exhausted from the years of being in that toxic relationship with him.

If you are dealing with a toxic relationship make the decision to do whatever it takes to focus on becoming a healthier you. The decision to love starts with you. You must first make the decision to love yourself. Build yourself up from the inside out. Speak life over yourself and commit to your own personal healing plan of self-care. It's mandatory that you commit to do whatever it takes to enjoy mental, spiritual and physical health.

You must become determined and motivated about your self-care. This is very important to enable you to build healthy relationships in your future. It starts with you. You must know that you deserve health, inner peace, love, and a sound mind.

The quality of your life relies on the quality of your communication with yourself. What you think, what you say and what you believe has a major impact on your relationship with God, yourself and others. How can you expect to have a successful marriage or friendship when you harbor negative thoughts and beliefs about yourself?

What's on the inside comes out. Inner bitterness, resentment and unhappy thoughts often manifest in the relationships you have with others. In life we often compare ourselves to others and we internalize feelings that we're not good enough or we settle and limit ourselves by making excuses. Instead of doing the necessary work we need to do by eating healthy, exercising, praying and filling our mind with positive thoughts we make excuses to why we can't. We think and say things like, "I don't have the time to exercise, or I don't have the money to buy healthy food or I don't have time to pray." Those excuses keep you stagnating in life.

Whether you're single or married I'm sure you can identify how you want your partner to be. Some people make lists of all the things they want in a mate and they are serious about that list;

- ✓ Tall
- ✓ Attractive
- ✓ Educated
- ✓ Financially stable
- ✓ Physically fit and healthy
- ✓ Etc. and the list goes on.

However, those same people who create lists of expectations for their ideal soul mate never create a list of goals for themselves.

Often times if they do, they don't actively pursue their personal goals, but they intently expect Mr. or Mrs. Right to be enamored with them.

It's not important what others think of you. What's important is what you think of yourself. The truth is, you will never truly respect and appreciate yourself if you never work on becoming better. Becoming all that you were created to be, starts with your mind.

"As a man thinks so is he" –Proverbs 23:7

You are your thoughts. Change your thoughts and you will change your life.

When it comes to relationships and handling disagreements there are several ways people deal with confrontation.

- ✓ They either shut down and decide not to share their thoughts or feelings in their attempt to avoid confrontation, which often leads to internal festering and a later outrageous outburst.
- ✓ Others decide to be more verbal and share too many feelings, which leads to emotions running wild with no understanding or attentive listening.

Both examples lead back to your communication with yourself. We all know money cannot create happiness. It's more the way you communicate with yourself about money that will create feelings of happiness. Being single or married doesn't creates happiness. It's what you communicate to yourself about your single or married status. Not even your spouse, partner or a family member can make you happy. It's what you communicate to yourself about your spouse or partner that can create unhappiness. You decide what thoughts you want to think; you decide what feelings you will allow. You can't change people, but when you make up your mind to change your thoughts you will change your life.

Your life is directly connected to your thoughts. Therefore, regardless of what you're going through in your life make the decision not to be the victim of your thoughts. Decide today to take full ownership of your healing. I want to also encourage you not to fall for the role of the savior. If you want to be a hero, save yourself. Rescue yourself from the toxic pattern of negative thinking. Detoxify your life from all the drama, lies, abuse and fear.

JOURNAL
———————— ✌︎☙✎❧ ————————

Can you relate to the victim and savior relationship?

_____

_____

_____

_____

_____

What are practical things you can start doing to enjoy mental, spiritual and physical health?

_____

_____

_____

_____

_____

"Being single or married doesn't create happiness, it's what you communicate to yourself about being single or married. You and only you are responsible for your happiness."

CHAPTER 4

————— ❧❦❧ —————

SHOULD YOU LEAVE OR SHOULD
YOU STAY

You may be wondering, is there hope? Can a frustrating, argumentative, painful relationship get better and become a healthy relationship? Can your partner change for the better? The answer is, yes. There is hope. Yes, it is possible for a stressful relationship to get better and become healthier. And yes, your partner can change.

However, this change for the better will require the full commitment and dedication from both you and your partner. The two of you must be determined to work on building a healthier relationship. If one person is fully committed and the other person is not committed it will not work out. It will take an effort from both of you. Understand that having a healthier relationship requires two individuals focusing together on becoming healthier people. If your partner denies his faults and refuses to work on changing for the better, that's a clear sign that the relationship will struggle. Don't be moved by spoken words, instead pay more attention to real actions. Actions always speak louder than words.

Every relationship goes through a test in difficult times. And the health of your relationship will always be determined by the resilience of both of you during the challenging seasons. Most couples make it through the wedding and honeymoon phase because those are the exciting and happy moments and times. But what about the seasons that put you through a trial? How will your relationship handle a job layoff or an ill relative? Will you support each other during the tough times? It's those difficult moments that will either strengthen or destroy your relationship; the way both of you handle them will determine your results. Your relationship is not a result of what happens to both of you. Your relationship is a result of how you both respond to what happens to you.

At the time of writing this book, my husband and I have been married for sixteen years. Throughout our sixteen years of our marriage we have encountered many challenging seasons. What I really love about our relationship is the mutual dedication we have to always improve. Even when disagreeing and we both felt like giving up, we committed to work on our personal growth. Sometimes it meant working with a therapist, attending a marriage retreat or working individually on our mental, physical and spiritual health. I can vouch after wanting to throw in the towel and deciding to instead use the challenge to grow we always reaped the rewards of an increase in love, intimacy, and deeper understanding after those difficult seasons.

Those who choose to give up never have the chance to experience the higher levels of love awaiting on the other side of the challenging uphill. Those who don't give up are rewarded abundantly. But it's not just about not giving up; you have to do the work. Stagnating and deciding to do nothing will bear no fruit. You will in fact automatically be in reverse gear when deciding to do nothing. You must be determined to do whatever it takes to get better regardless how hard the effort and the challenge to obtain your goal. We are created to evolve, anything in your life that's not evolving is bound to fail. Always ask the question, "How can we evolve?"

In the current season of your relationship you may be asking, "Should I stay or should I go?" You need to consider the following things when deciding if you should stay in or leave a relationship?

- If you or your partner is not willing to consider personal growth and actively working to change for the better, ask yourself if you are willing to make the sacrifice required to continue in a failing relationship?

  If the relationship has significant trust issues that the two of you don't want to work on towards healing (like infidelity), you may want to consider closing the chapter. The truth is some people are not prepared to discipline themselves to be part of a monogamous relationship. Instead of worrying yourself sick every moment of the day whether or not your partner is going to be faithful, relieve yourself from the mental stress by removing yourself from the relationship. Do what's best for your overall health.

- Trust your intuition. At the end of the day the answer lies within you and it's important that you accept and embrace the truth. Although the truth will hurt in the beginning, truth triumphs in the end.

- Make an assessment of your desires. Where do you really see yourself three years from now? Do you see a future with your partner? Can you envision the two of you growing old together?

- Get clear on why it's difficult to make a decision. Are you feeling guilty about something? Do you struggle with a low self-esteem? Make sure your decisions come from a healthy place.

In my book "Addicted to Pain: Renew Your Mind and Heal Your Spirit from a Toxic Relationship In 30 Days," I wrote about letting go and surrendering. Here's an excerpt from the book:

"Create a plan of no personal contact with your ex. I understand that this may be difficult, but it's very necessary for your healing process. This is possible even if the two of you have kids. You will simply start to treat your ex like a coworker or business partner and nothing more. You want to be sure to respect each other for the kids' sake but avoid any and all conversations that aren't about your children.

If you don't have children, delete your ex's contact information, block his phone number and remove his ability to contact you through social media and messaging outlets. It's very important that you make a deliberate break in order to heal. When past lovers fail to let go completely, they often relapse and find themselves going back and forth with each other, piling more hurt, confusion and heartbreak onto wounds that never had a chance to heal.

You may be thinking, "I can't just let go. It's too difficult. I still love him." Even if you truly love him, you can let go, and you will with the grace and power of God. Unconditional love does not mean you should accept unconditional behavior. If you really love him, let him go. And if the love is real, it will come back after the healing process. Don't continue to spend your life in a toxic relationship because you're too emotional and needy to let go. Remember, you can do all things through Christ. Ask the Holy Spirit to strengthen you and empower you to let go. If you don't let go, it's going to be very difficult to heal."

I would like to add additional advice to the no contact rule. If you are dealing with a very manipulative person who calls you several times a days and uses your children to control you, block them and remove all the access they have to you. If they want to see your children tell them to contact your parents or someone else you trust who can act as the middle person between you and your ex. There's no valid reason for them having access to you at all, and especially not several times a day. It can be draining, toxic and soul-sucking. Remove all their privileges to have contact with you and take time to heal. Remember your mental, emotional and physical health is very important. Make yourself a priority and heal. As you progress in self-love you will begin to understand more and more that everyone should not have the rights to access you. Guard your heart and protect your peace.

Stay Focused

Commit your actions to the Lord, and your plans will succeed. (Proverbs 16:3) God has created each of us for a particular purpose in life and it is our responsibility to maintain focus on fulfilling that purpose. There are visions, plans and ideas in everyone that God intended to be executed through and to each person. It is therefore important to maintain focus.

Often, we are distracted by the challenges that we face in life. This causes us to occasionally lose our focus in relationships or lose our focus to be able to receive a relationship. Relationships are not something someone can just go out and grab, but you must be focused enough to receive the person God intended you to connect with and have a committed successful relationship as a result.

To befittingly receive your partner, you must maintain a clear focus. Understand that receiving a relationship is more than simply making a catch. It means accepting your partner and being willing to embrace the God given differences created inside both of you. The decision to receive the relationship God intended you to have must be made daily. Each day you should be reminded that a relationship means that you are on the same team and that your differences will collectively contribute to the success of your relationship and family.

In relationships, the ultimate goal should be to reflect the image of God through your relationship and family. Therefore, you cannot afford to waste time being distracted and disconnected from your future success.

Mark 11:24 (NIV) - Therefore I tell you, whatever you ask for in prayer, believe that you have received it, and it will be yours.

Colossians 3:23-24 (NIV) - Whatever you do, work at it with all your heart, as working for the Lord, not for human masters, since you know that you will receive an inheritance from the Lord as a reward. It is the Lord Christ you are serving.

While my wife and I were dating, we would spend countless hours on the phone. We would discuss from our thoughts and desires we wanted in a relationship to our career aspirations. As we continued to talk, we grew in our understanding of each other and had a better sense of how our relationship could be in the future.

During this time, I was given a vision. The vision took place in the future of my life. I was walking into the family room of my home. The wall was decorated with picture frames, however there were no pictures in the frames. From a distance every picture in the frames looked like a solid black patch. As I walked closer to the frames, I could see the image of a family, but without any visible faces as the faces were blurred. I continued to walk closer and the faces slowly started coming into focus and taking shape. Once standing directly in front of the frames, the once solid black image clearly took the shape of a picture of myself, my wife and our future family.

After having had this vision, I wrote it down and later communicated it to my then girlfriend. She received it with joy, the same joy I already experienced. Accordingly, that which we received with focus and clarity would soon become our reality and we were married shortly after.

Follow your God-given vision.

JOURNAL

Most couples make it through the wedding and honeymoon phase because those are the exciting and happy moments and times. But what about the seasons that put you through a trial? How will your relationship survive the challenging times?

_____

_____

_____

_____

_____

Do you see a future with your partner? Can you envision the two of you growing old together?

_____

_____

_____

_____

_____

"Receiving your relationship is more than just being with someone but it means accepting them and being willing to embrace the God-given differences created inside both of you."

CHAPTER 5

⁓⁓⁓

THE PAIN OF TAKING THINGS PERSONALLY

There was a time in my life when I was very sensitive and vulnerable to the opinions of others. I would get my feelings hurt a lot. I would become resentful of small petty remarks made by certain relatives and I would often cry uncontrollably when my husband offended me with his words. For years I suffered for the sake of seeking the approval, acceptance and validation of others. I took every criticism and negative opinion people had about me personally until I learned how to gain control over my emotions.

During the season when I learned this valuable lesson I was also tested. This was during the most difficult time in my marriage. Both of us just went through a major loss. We lost family, we lost our home, we lost money and we felt like we were losing each other. During this season in my life I felt like everything was being attacked. I felt attacked in my mind, body and spirit. I wrote about this in more detail in my book "Miracles in Your Mouth," so I won't tell the entire story again. However, we were at a breaking point and our marriage was suffering. I felt tested to really put into practice the principal of not taking things personally when for the first time (after about 13 years of marriage) my husband told me he wasn't happy and considering a divorce. The little girl in me who needed the approval and validation from others wanted to cry, scream and run away. The arrogant ego in me wanted revenge and considered punishing him by withdrawing mentally and physically. But the healthy, wise, understanding, and new powerful woman I was becoming decided not to take his words personally.

When I heard him say he was unhappy and considering a divorce, I immediately spoke to myself. I didn't speak out loud. I spoke to my inner self. My inner voice spoke loudly throughout my spirit, saying, "Rainie don't you dare get emotional. His feelings of being unhappy and wanting to leave has nothing to do with you. Those are his feelings alone and he has a right to express his feelings. But clearly understand this, him expressing those feeling is not supposed to control how you feel. You are overcoming depression, panic attacks and other health issues. Rainie, you cannot afford to allow anyone to trigger those toxic emotions in your life. You are not a victim; you are powerful and strong, and you can overcome this. You will overcome this. Understand that he's hurting and he's simply expressing that hurt. However, that hurt that he's expressing does not define who you are. Do not feel sorry for yourself. You are loved, you are powerful, and you are coming out stronger." My inner spirit spoke life and power over me while I was experiencing one of the toughest times in my life. And the decision I made not to take things personally was what helped me evolve into a healthier, happier and more fulfilled person.

It was amazing. I watched myself become the powerful strong woman I always desired to be. I refused to be controlled by another person's words and feelings. I took full responsibility and control of my own emotions. It was so liberating, and life has only gotten better and better.

"You never know how strong you are until being strong is your only choice." -Bob Marley

No matter what another person does to you, do not take it personally. What people do to you is not because of you. People are a reflection of their own thoughts and their actions are based on their perception and view of life. When you take what they do or say personally you're assuming they understand and view life the same way you do. We are all living in our own world with our own unique experiences and points of view.

When you take what another person says or does personally, you make it easy for the behavior of people to control you mentally and emotionally. You are giving people power and control when you decide to internalize another person's actions as a personal offense towards you.

When you make the decision not to take things personally, you can live your life with an uncluttered heart. You can love freely without fear of rejection. No one can hurt you because you are living with a deep understanding that what people do has nothing to do with you personally. You are never responsible for the decisions of others. You are only responsible for yourself.

We were able to heal during that season in our marriage, because we both allowed each other to express our truths and not take it personally. Prior to getting to that place of healing we felt depleted. We had lost ourselves in marriage, parenting and our careers. We didn't know how to really enjoy life as individuals. The titles of Mr. and Mrs. and dad and mom had become our identity. We were both unfulfilled and unhappy. We made the decision to work through our healing process by creating new health and fitness habits. We invested in therapy, building healthier communication habits and working on becoming healthy and whole individuals who focused more on self-care. All of these things were very important to our health and they enhanced our marriage tremendously.

Raise Your Standards

Have you ever heard the saying 90% of being a good father is being there? I have. I have seen memes about it and even Father's Day messages congratulating fathers on being present in the lives of their families. For example, a picture of a father walking along-side a son on his bike as he presumably learns how to ride it without training wheels. This picture says it all. Not just the picture but the words that summarize the important fact that Fathers should just be there.

Some of the most well-intentioned messages like this one can be misleading. Many of us have witnessed families of single parent homes, so the idea of being there makes sense. It makes sense to believe that being there is enough. However, for well-intentioned fathers who are "there" to partly fulfill this prophecy, any challenging words or comments requesting more actions, criticizing remarks or ill formatted words of "encouragement" can create frustration and anger. This frustration and anger come from taking those words personally; the act of internalizing spoken words as a personal attack on one's character or presence. Holding on too tight to the idea that 90% of being a good father is being there, while facing criticism, can result in frustration. Similar to Ralphie, in the movie "A Christmas Story" being so happy to turn in his report on what he wanted for Christmas, only to receive a C+. And to make matters worse, while you're in this state of feeling like your efforts aren't appreciated, you are then hit in the face with a "snowball sandwich" by a situation you thought was already dealt with. At this point the rage boils over and in the words of Tyreese you scream "What more do you want from ME!"

That was me. I would regard me being present in the lives of my family as one of the most valuable parts of being a good man, husband and father. I took the sheer mention of anything I should work on to improve as a personal attack. If I was told, "We don't spend enough time together," I would think and sometimes say, "I'm here and we are together all the time. Do you not appreciate me coming home at a decent time from work?" If she would say, "We haven't been talking much," my mental response was "I just talked to you and you seemed just fine. Do you not appreciate me answering the phone every time you call me?" In my mind the mention of what was not being done was irrelevant because I had known and seen so many couples and men that have done much less. In my mind, I was doing all that was required, and any complaint or critical compliment was taken out of context and regarded as a personal attack and a lack of appreciation.

Over time, I would realize that the act of internalizing comments and taking comments personally was detrimental to your mental health. Not only does it lead to constant arguments but also resentment from feeling your actions are not appreciated. Where was this coming from? I knew that some of the things said weren't a reflection of who I am.

However, the fear of someone else believing I was whatever was being said, along with wanting to be right/justified, caused frustration. I had to recognize that the frustration I felt was from me drawing conclusions from what I've heard, instead of listening to understand what was being communicated. I realized I had given the power of how I feel away to others. Not only was I taking things personally, but I would ponder over them minute after minute.

I had to come to terms with what was going on and take back the power to control my emotions. I began to meditate on non-reactivity, constantly reminding myself of the scripture to think only upon things that are of positive report. (Philippians 4:8)

Throughout this process, I had to remind myself to get a grip on any negative thoughts and redirect those thoughts. In this process and over time I became better at witnessing what was taking place in my mind and instead of getting wrapped up in those emotions, I could now identify their presence and redirect them instead.

The act of redirecting my thoughts and renewing my mind has been a journey. And I know that if I can change and challenge my own thoughts anyone can. Understand that your thoughts are a reflection of the world we are raised in. However, we are not powerless to the ideas and thoughts of the world around us. We have the power to disconnect from the world around us and transform our minds to operate in a manner reflecting who we truly are. Who we are is what truly matters. A key to be the best husband, father or overall person is being able to know who you are. Do your best to remind yourself of who God created you to be. Don't allow the ideas of this world and the words of people around you to cause you to personalize and internalize things in a negative way and create limitations in your life. Take the time to do the internal work and avoid the trap of self-sabotage, pride and prejudice by taking things personally.

After doing so, you become alive in a way you have never known before. And with this new mindset, you can then move forward in raising your standards and challenging yourself to be a better man, woman, husband, wife, father, mother and parent in a loving relationship.

The key to this is moving beyond the norm of negativity and not being mentally saturated by standards so low that you give yourself a pat on the back for being present. You being a better you and striving to be a better partner has more to do with your own visions and goals than comparing yourself to the negative statistics regarding failed relationships. So instead of taking it personally when someone is asking more of you, beyond your physical presence, embrace it as an opportunity to become better. Never allow the norms of your upbringing to determine your willingness to pursue being the best you possibly can be. If you were raised in a fatherless home, separated family or have seen ongoing toxic relationships, don't lower your own standards. Don't allow those experiences to be your point of reference as to how you ought to live your life. Go beyond your norms and know that you can decide to love better, communicate better and think better because your standards aren't set by who others are, but they are set by who God called you to be. Focus on these questions: How can I be better? How can I love better? And how I can I create better intimacy beyond what I have experienced before.

JOURNAL

What did your parents (and other relationships you encountered in your life) teach you about love?

_____

_____

_____

_____

_____

How can you become intentional about not allowing the negative relationship examples influence you to lower your standards in your relationship?

_____

_____

_____

_____

_____

"When you decide not to take things personally, you love freely, and no one can hurt you because you understand that what people do has nothing to do with you personally."

CHAPTER 6

⊱❦⊰

SPEAK LIFE OVER YOUR RELATIONSHIP

There is power in your words. What you say will eventually direct your actions, behavior, habits and ultimately your life. If you want to change anything in your life one of the most powerful mind programming strategies is the use of auto-suggestion. Auto-suggestion is another term for speaking affirmations. It is the process of using your words to create change in your behavior. Whether you realize it or not you have been using auto-suggestion. Think about it, have you ever said, "I'm so tired or I don't have any energy." Have you also noticed after saying that you felt even more tired and feeling tired and depleted of energy felt like a normal state of being? That's an example of the power of auto-suggestion. People are often using auto-suggestion subconsciously unaware of its effects on their lives. Your entire life starts with your thoughts and your words give life to those thoughts which ultimately creates the outcomes of your life through your actions and beliefs. When you really understand this, you will no longer blame others for the outcomes in your life.

Auto-suggestion can be used to transform any area of your life including your relationship. Now, don't get me wrong I'm not claiming that you can change another person or control them with auto-suggestion. Auto-suggestion is a personal practice to change you. Changing you for the better will benefit all your relationships. As you change your thoughts, words and beliefs to be more positive you will have a more positive view of others including your relationship.

Am I promising you will live happily ever after with your partner after you start practicing auto-suggestion? No, I am not promising you that. However, when you focus more on becoming a healthier and happier you, there's a good chance you may influence your partner to use some of those healthier habits or they may not desire a healthier lifestyle altogether. One thing is for sure, you will start to attract more positive people and even people who are inspired to live positive lives. The main point is you focusing on being a better you and letting go of the need to drag your partner along or force him/her to change. Understand that this is your season to act on; a season to consistently invest in your mind, body and spirit. Focus more on shining your light, being an example of positive change and being patient with your partner by understanding everyone has their own life to live and challenges to overcome. It's never your job to control or manipulate your partner to do things your way even if you know it's what will be best for him/her.

As you start speaking life over yourself, you will begin to develop and grow your faith. The more you believe in your words the more your actions will follow that belief and your life will begin to manifest in a new positive reality created by your consistent dedication to becoming a better you.

The following are affirmations (auto-suggestions) you may utilize to start declaring life over your relationship:

- ❖ I only attract healthy and happy relationships
- ❖ I am so happy and grateful to give and receive love
- ❖ My relationship is joyous and I'm happily in love
- ❖ I have the power to create my own happiness
- ❖ God is connecting me to loyal loving relationships

Feeling Like Giving Up

Have you ever felt unprepared to be in a committed relationship? Have you ever told yourself, "I'm not ready to settle down, I still have some 'living' to do and things to learn?" Have you ever said, "I'll get married when I get older and I'm established in my career?" Many times, we are chatting ourselves into ideas about relationships that hinder us from being able to successfully manage one. If we surprisingly meet someone and start a serious relationship, our prior thoughts of not being ready will eventually seek expression in some way in the future. Therefore, it is important to watch what we speak over ourselves. With our thoughts, we have the power to create limitations, establish expectations and influence our outcomes in various situations in life and relationships.

One evening, I met up with an old friend from high school for happy hour, George. George and I hadn't seen each other in years but we remained connected through life's changes via Facebook and Instagram. Following our high school graduation, George attended Hampton University in Virginia to study business where he met his wife during their junior year. They were married a year later. When we were college students, we would occasionally talk, and he would mention to me the reason he was going to school for business was because he felt he couldn't work for anyone long term. He would always say, "If I need a job, I must create one because I cannot work for someone else and make them rich." Year after year he would tell me this. Not only did he say it, but it was also seen in his career history throughout college. George never worked any job longer than 8 to 9 months. I recall during his junior year of college, he shocked us all by working at Subway for nearly 12 months before deciding that the franchise owner reaped too much benefit from his culinary artistry, sandwich making skills, and that he would be better off pursuing his own business and becoming a full-time entrepreneur.

Upon graduation from college, George with the support of his wife, decided to start an In-Home Health Care Agency. George focused on the business full-time while his wife worked as a marketing associate at a local investment firm. Over the course of 6 years, the business had gradually grown to earning them close to six-figures in profits. At this point, George decided he wanted to expand his business to his hometown to be closer to family. So roughly 7 years following college graduation, George and his family, which now included his wife and two children, decided to move back to our hometown of St. Louis, Missouri to start the new business. His wife landed a job as a marketing manager at a St. Louis investment firm, so she had no initial issues with the move.

We talked occasionally, but now that years had gone by since he moved back, this is our first time in a while catching up with each other. Shortly after sitting down, I asked, "How have you been, I see your business is going great and family is looking good." He briefly smiled and said, "Thanks bro," as he grabbed one of the buffalo wings from his plate. Shortly after swallowing his first bite, he said, "Bro, I need your advice." I said, "Sure, what's up?" He explained to me how the government changed its regulations and how it impacted his business. Basically, his business was operating at a loss. As a matter of fact, his business has been operating at a loss for the past few years. He explained that he thought that his move to St. Louis would open opportunities for his business because the Virginia market was saturated. However, the move did not and the lack of business had an impact on his relationship with his wife. He communicated that they argue all the time and he was confused about what to do. Honestly, he didn't know what to do about their relationship and as a reminder he informed me that, "You know I can't work for anyone either, so I don't know what to do about the business either." Therefore, he was doing nothing, not working on the business, neither working on his relationship. He was going about his daily routine as if nothing should be changed. For the business he took out loans to pay payroll, while using the same debt to purchase items he could no longer afford, only to later post them on Instagram to impress his followers. He was stuck. Stuck in the routine he had created. He didn't imagine things could be this hard in his relationship. And to worsen matters, his wife demanded he figure things out with the business or get a job and she even talked about divorce.

What George didn't realize was that every word spoken by him based on the feelings he had created apathy in his life and relationship. Apathy meaning, he had given up. Now that things were hard, instead of looking for ways to overcome them, he complained that things shouldn't be this hard in the first place. And instead of working on his relationship, he decided to take trips with his friends, leaving his wife and kids to figure things out on their own. Not only were his thoughts keeping him stuck but the words he spoke were words of failure that limited his ability to positively impact his life and relationship.

Whether we acknowledge it or not, most of the time our thoughts create the stumbling blocks in front of ourselves, which make it a challenge to overcome adversity. We chat ideas into our own heads over and over to the point where they become automatic suggestions that subconsciously control our lives. It is hence important to be aware of the words we speak over ourselves about ourselves. We must speak life over our situation and affirm the possibilities of generating the outcome we strive for in our lives. And then take the necessary steps to progressively create the events needed to change our lives.

The act of affirming positivity in your thoughts is the process of renewing your mind. Never let the thoughts and ideas of your past, or even your present, prevent you from being willing to be patient with the challenges that life brings. Instead focus on having the fortitude to persevere in your moments of weakness. Life is full of temptations; temptations of believing challenges are too hard and temptations of believing there is no hope. A key to overcoming these actions is to first of all acknowledge the presence of these temptations. After acknowledgement of what is taking place, you now have the power to resist that temptation by doing what may be easy and what you may want to do, but instead doing what you have to do to overcome that challenge. In relationships though it may come naturally to do what you want to do. You however create more value as a spouse by doing what needs to be done.

With that in mind here are keys I've provided to overcoming these types of challenges. First, take responsibility for the outcome of your desire. Often, we blame others and external events as the reason for our failures or challenges and overlook how we have contributed to the failure. We overlook the words we speak and the thoughts we have, which also impact our outcomes. And even though it may be hard to accept, even in cases where someone else is responsible for the fault, it is our responsibility to change. And we must take the necessary action to fix whatever is broken.

Secondly, don't allow success or failure to determine how you feel about yourself. Never add too much value to the things you do to make yourself feel valuable. Life is about who you are, not what you know or what you do for a living. Lastly, whatever place you may find yourself in, if you don't have the tools, spend some time getting spiritual clarity. You can do this through prayer, meditation and connecting with your intuition. Trust that God will provide the divine assistance needed to get the job done. There may be times when the education you received is not 100% applicable when you actually get the job. Most of the time, becoming fully educated requires on the job training. Never be too proud to learn on the fly. Be humble enough to admit, although I don't know what to do right now, I am willing to learn and try my best to create the vision I have for my life and family.

JOURNAL

Have you ever felt unprepared to be in a committed relationship?

_____

_____

_____

_____

_____

Are you telling yourself things about your relationship that is hindering you from being able to successfully manage your emotions?

_____

_____

_____

_____

_____

"Changing you for the better can benefit your relationship for the better."

CHAPTER 7

—————— ❦❧ ——————

ACCEPTANCE AND
UNCONDITIONAL LOVE

For years in my marriage I would complain to my husband about the things I wanted him to change. I would complain he wasn't spending enough time with me. I would complain he wasn't helping to keep the house clean. And I would complain he was not speaking up for me when dealing with in-laws. Sometimes I would get very emotional about these things and I would internalize them as if they were a reflection of how he felt about me. Nothing was good enough. I could easily find a reason to become upset with him and complain.

The arguments and complaints became a pattern in my life until I discovered the power of acceptance and unconditional love. What I've discovered is that true acceptance and unconditional love first starts with me. I had to first learn to fully accept and love myself unconditionally before I could really understand and know how to fully accept and love my husband unconditionally. This process started through a daily self-care practice that included meditation, affirmations and exercise. The more I spoke life over myself, the more I believed in myself and the more I began to accept and love myself. The more I did this the more I grew in my capacity to love and accept others, especially my husband. This daily practice caused me to feel better about life. And instead of complaining and focusing on what was wrong I began focusing on everything that was right and even speaking words of positivity. I started speaking life over my husband. I started to affirm how much I appreciated him and believed in him. I would send him daily text messages that read;

"Good morning my amazing, handsome, strong, sexy King. I love you so much, have a wonderful day."

In the beginning these text messages felt weird. I was not used to speaking positive things like this to my husband, especially not consistently. I knew I loved and appreciated him, but I never felt it was necessary to send daily messages affirming it. I definitely could not remember ever calling him my king. It almost felt like speaking a foreign language. Then eventually the more I sent the positive affirming text messages the more it felt normal and when we would see each other at home the energy between us was much more positive. He would send me messages saying, "Good morning my beautiful, amazing, sexy smart Queen, I love you."

As I spoke to the king in him, he spoke to the queen in me and we both grew in our respect, acceptance and unconditional love. Our powerful positive words enhanced our relationship more and more. We started seeing the greatness in each other. My husband began to reflect every positive affirmation I spoke over him. He treated me like a queen, and he carried himself more like a king in everything he did. Our relationship blossomed more than ever before. Our passion and excitement for each other was strengthened. We started working together in a more peaceful and united way. We started performing better in accomplishing our relationship, parenting, and business goals. We viewed each other differently. Instead of arguing and seeing each other as divided, we saw each other in a more supportive way. Whenever we had a disagreement we understood that we were not enemies but we were on the same team and our goal was to work together towards the enhancement of our family.

This has become so powerful in our relationship and whenever we sensed the arguments or critical conversations coming up, we stepped in to take corrective actions. Sometimes in the middle of an argument or disagreement, we would stop and address the core issue (whether it was a lack of appreciation or feeling judged) and affirmed our love and appreciation for each other. We understood the importance of physical and emotional intimacy in marriage and always made time for deep connections especially during busy seasons when we felt more disconnected.

As we evolved in our marriage we understood it was an ongoing process of commitment and consistently building each other up. We knew that we were not perfect and our work did not stop. We were to never become idol in our pursuit to grow in our love and acceptance for each other. We are still growing. It's important to never stop doing what's necessary in our love relationship even when it requires from us to be more humble, submissive and also when it's necessary to speak to the greatness inside of each other even when we don't feel like it. Love is a decision not a feeling.

Unconditional Love

What is unconditional love? Is it the ability to forgive someone when they mistreat or offend you? Is it the ability to be there for someone in their time of need? Or is it the act of staying with a person through sickness, health, wealth or poverty? When I reflect on what it means to love unconditionally, I am reminded of a Bible scripture.

"But God showed His great love for us by sending Christ to die for us while we were still sinners (Romans 5:8)."

Have you ever wondered why God didn't wait for us to have things all together before He sent Christ into the world? I believe it is because God saw what He originally created in man and saw beyond the sin and looking at the initial goodness He beheld that day of creation. And because God saw beyond our sin and saw our purpose, His great love wouldn't allow Him to sit idle and not provide a solution.

Often the lens through which we see ourselves and others is a reflection of our life experiences, both positive and negative. This effects how we honor and love ourselves and each other. Because of this, our expression of "love" can at times be conditional and based on what others say, do and even how we feel. Does this mean we are called to endure toxic relationships and subject ourselves to the bad decisions of others? No. I would not dare recommend anyone endure such abusive treatment. Nor should anyone make excuses for someone consistently making bad choices.

However, we can accept a person for whom he/she is, see the God in them and yet determine how we ought to show love. Whether its love up close or love from a distance.

Ultimately, to fully love unconditionally we must look beyond external expressions, pet peeves we dislike in a person or the temporary happiness that comes from receiving a nice gift from someone. We must see the God in them and who God created them to be.

When we activate the ability to see each other in a positive light, even though we know we are imperfect and make mistakes, we activate our acceptance of flaws and the ability to express love regardless of circumstances. I am often reminded of this by members of my family. Though some may have alcohol-related drinking problems, opioid addictions or failed marriages because of bad decisions they've made; I can make the decision to love the person and not the dysfunction.

Taking a deeper look at someone to identify their good internal attributes is not an easy thing to do. This is still a struggle. It's never easy to forgive flaws and offenses to accept and love someone. It is something that should be worked on constantly. Understand that this inner work is for you to fulfill. It's really not about fixing others, changing their behavior or making them see where they are wrong, but it is to release you from being part of that same toxic energy. Instead, you are taking back your power and not allowing the actions of others to dictate your capacity to love. Though things may not be ideal in your relationship, you have the power to make the decision to love anyway. And as it relates to maintaining a lifelong committed relationship, it can only be done when two people have decided to love each other regardless of their imperfections. Each person must ask themselves, "How can I love more?" "How can I grow in my capacity to love?" And after that, make the decision to face and overcome the challenges of life that makes it easy not to love. Despite everything going on around you. make the decision to love.

Love never gives up, never loses faith, is always hopeful, and endures through every circumstance (1 Cor. 13:7).

Decide to Love.

JOURNAL

How can you grow in your capacity to love?

_____

_____

_____

_____

_____

What are the important decisions you will make to enjoy a
healthy relationship?

_____

_____

_____

_____

_____

"You can accept who a person is, see the God in them and yet determine how you ought to show love. Whether it's love up close or love from a distance…"

CONCLUSION

———— ❧❦❧❦ ————

Understand that there's great purpose and divine connections in your life. Pay attention to the inner guidance from your spirit. Healthy relationships bring feelings of safety, love and acceptance. They should not cause you to feel tense, fearful and anxious. As you grow in your capacity to love, remember to protect your peace and stay away from anyone who tries to make you feel bad for making yourself a priority. Self love is not selfish. It doesn't matter what people say about you, what's important is what you say about you. Your thoughts of yourself are much more powerful than the thoughts others have of you. When you make the decision to let go of everything that is not divinely designed for you, you set yourself up for receipt of your purpose. What God has for you is for you. You don't have to force anything, you don't have to beg or cry out loud for it. You will discover that some of the most peaceful moments of life is when you find the courage to let go of what you can't change. The reason some people don't heal is because they keep replaying painful scenarios in their heads. Let it go. You are only one decision away from a totally amazing life. Make the decision to move forward with a new attitude, new mindset and new positive expectations. Don't allow people to pick and choose if or when they'll treat you right. Deciding to love is also making the decision to guard your heart and protect your peace.

"Love is not a feeling; Love is a decision."

ARE YOU ADDICTED TO A TOXIC LOVE?

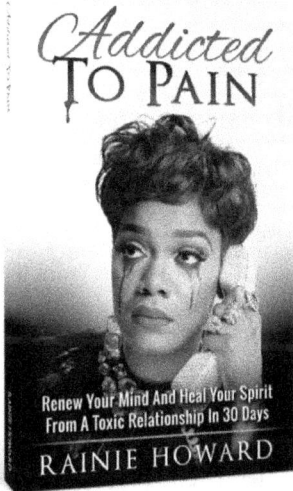

The obsession of a toxic relationship can have the same enticement as drugs or alcohol. The pattern echoes time and time again: a new significant other draws you into a new relationship that starts off lovingly and alluringly only to develop into a hurtful or abusive cycle. A person with a healthy understanding of "true love" do not tolerate this kind of pain. He or she will move on in search of a healthier bond. It's an unhealthy view of love that will rationalize in toxic behavior and make another person cling to a relationship long after it should have ended. Like any other addiction, those hooked on toxic love have little or no control over excessive urges to text, call, manipulate or beg for love, attention and affection. They want help. They want to end the pain and recover, but it's much like trying to shake a drug habit. Get your copy at http://bit.ly/AddictedToPain

Have you been trapped in a constant cycle of toxic relationships that have you frustrated with your love life?

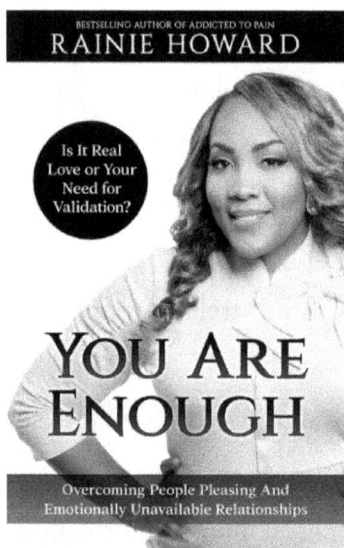

Do you feel fear, insecurity and anxiety that have you asking yourself 'Am I enough?'

You Are Enough takes readers on an incredible journey of self-understanding to explore the root causes of negative emotions projecting themselves in their outside relationships.

The concept that the fear of never finding true love and consistently trying to please others are major factors for the engagement in toxic relationships. By addressing the fear and anxiety you feel inside, Rainie helps you discover your true self-worth, which is sure to change your life!

Get your copy at http://bit.ly/YouAreEnoughBook

HAVE YOU BEEN PRAYING FOR A HUSBAND?

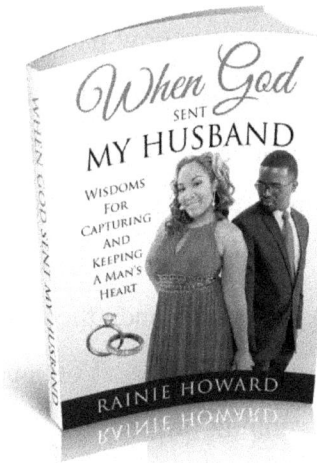

It's not easy being single, and when you have a vision to be married, it's challenging to patiently wait for the right one. It's important to understand that God has a divine purpose for your life, and He wants to gift you with the right man. *When God Sent My Husband* is a single women's guide to gaining wisdom on:

- How to guard your heart yet freely love
- Preparing and positioning yourself to receive love
- Building a solid foundation that captures and sustains love

In this book, Rainie Howard shares her personal story of searching for love, dating and embracing the divine experience of God bringing her husband into her life. This is a miraculous story of God being the ultimate matchmaker. The book will encourage you to take a spiritual approach towards dating and preparing for marriage. Get your copy at http://bit.ly/WhenGodSentMyHusband

EVER FELT STUCK OR WEIGHTED DOWN BY THE PRESSURES OF LIFE?

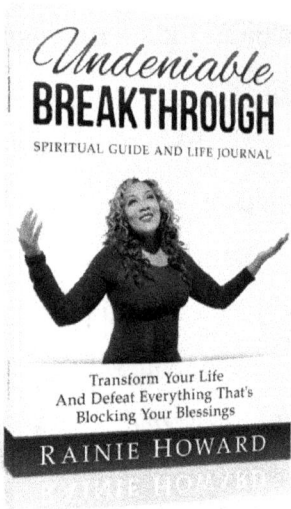

Undeniable
BREAKTHROUGH
SPIRITUAL GUIDE AND LIFE JOURNAL

Transform Your Life
And Defeat Everything That's
Blocking Your Blessings

RAINIE HOWARD

No matter how hard you try, you just can't get unstuck. It's like sitting in a car, pushing down on the accelerator as hard as you can, and the car never moving. You are running in the race of life, but you're getting nowhere. Doors are constantly closing, opportunities are nowhere to be found, and you can't get your breakthrough. You've tried everything, but nothing seems to work. You are in desperate need of an "Undeniable Breakthrough!" Whether you need a breakthrough in your relationship, career, finances or health, this spiritual guide will give you all the life strategies needed to experience the blessings of an undeniable breakthrough. Get your copy at http://bit.ly/UndeniableBreakthrough

Did you know that anxiety, depression, and fear stem from emotional experiences you keep tucked away in your heart?

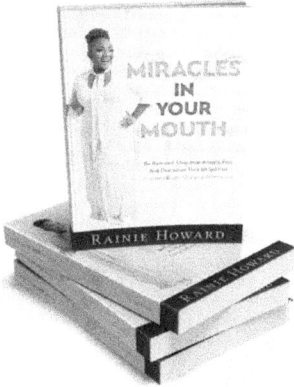

Often, people who struggle with anxiety, depression, worry, and fear are left with a sense of hopelessness. They become entangled in a battle against their own emotions, giving way to confusion, stress, and even panic attacks. As isolation sets in, it's whispering doubts make people believe they are alone, misunderstood, and sometimes even unloved. The good news is you can find hope and healing in life's darkest moments. In Miracles In Your Mouth, you will learn the spiritual strategy to heal, renew, and transform your life. God wants to unleash His power, protection, and prosperity upon you. Will you accept it? Bestselling author Rainie Howard shares the mysteries of covenant prayer, powerful affirmations, and divine declarations to strengthen your mind, heal your emotions, and renew your spirit.

Get your copy at www.MiraclesInYourMouth.com